EARLY SCIENCE

LIQUID

KIM THOMPSON

A Crabtree Roots Book

Crabtree Publishing
crabtreebooks.com

School-to-Home Support for Caregivers and Teachers

This book helps children grow by letting them practice reading. Here are a few guiding questions to help the reader with building his or her comprehension skills. Possible answers appear here in red.

Before Reading:

• What do I think this book is about?
  - *I think this book is about water.*
  - *I think this book is about playing in water.*

• What do I want to learn about this topic?
  - *I want to learn what* liquid *means.*
  - *I want to learn how to tell the difference between a liquid and something else.*

During Reading:

• I wonder why...
  - *I wonder how many things around me are liquids.*
  - *I wonder what other kinds of matter there can be.*

• What have I learned so far?
  - *I have learned that liquids take the shape of whatever container they are in.*
  - *I have learned that you can weigh a liquid.*

After Reading:

• What details did I learn about this topic?
  - *I have learned that I drink liquids.*
  - *I have learned that rain is liquid water.*

• Read the book again and look for the vocabulary words.
  - *I see the word **matter** on page 3 and the word **liquid** on page 4. The other vocabulary words are found on page 14.*

All things are **matter**.

lemonade

Some matter is **liquid**.

water

juice

A liquid has **weight**.

A liquid can change its **shape**.

A liquid takes the shape of its **container**.

Rain is liquid water.

Is water always a liquid?

How could you change it?

Word List
Sight Words

a	has	takes
all	is	the
are	its	things
can	of	water
change	some	

Words to Know

container

liquid

matter

rain

shape

weight

30 Words

All things are **matter**.

Some matter is **liquid**.

A liquid has **weight**.

A liquid can change its **shape**.

A liquid takes the shape of its **container**.

Rain is liquid water.

Written by: Kim Thompson

Designed by: Rhea Wallace

Series Development: James Earley

Proofreader: Kathy Middleton

Educational Consultant: Marie Lemke M.Ed.

Photographs:
Shutterstock: Ittipon: cover; JenniFoto: p. 1; Sergey
    Novikov: p. 3, 14-15; Eastimages: p. 7; Vach
    Cameraman: p. 9; Robert Kneschke: p. 10; SongPin:
    p. 13

Crabtree Publishing

crabtreebooks.com   800-387-7650
Copyright © 2024 Crabtree Publishing

Printed in Canada/112023/20231130

Published in Canada
Crabtree Publishing
616 Welland Ave.
St. Catharines, Ontario
L2M 5V6

Published in the United States
Crabtree Publishing
347 Fifth Ave
Suite 1402-145
New York, NY 10016

Library and Archives Canada Cataloguing in Publication
Available at Library and Archives Canada

Library of Congress Cataloging-in-Publication Data
Available at the Library of Congress

Hardcover: 978-1-0398-0970-3
Paperback: 978-1-0398-1023-5
Ebook (pdf): 978-1-0398-1129-4
Epub: 978-1-0398-1076-1